W9-DIS-891

All-Time Favorites No. 109

# Scott Joplin

## PIANO MUSIC

**CONTENTS**

**CARL FISCHER, Inc.**
62 COOPER SQUARE, NEW YORK 10003
BOSTON · CHICAGO · LOS ANGELES

Copyright © 1985 by Carl Fischer, Inc.
62 Cooper Square, New York, NY 10003
*International Copyright Secured.*
All rights reserved including performing rights.
Printed in the U.S.A.

ISBN 0-8258-0378-0

# Maple Leaf Rag

SCOTT JOPLIN

**Tempo di marcia.**

# The Entertainer
## A Ragtime Two-Step

SCOTT JOPLIN

**INTRO:**
*Not fast.*

Repeat 8va.

# The Easy Winners
## A Ragtime Two-Step

SCOTT JOPLIN

*Introduction.*
*Not fast.*

# The Cascades
## A Rag

SCOTT JOPLIN

*Tempo di Marcia.*

16

# Peacherine Rag

SCOTT JOPLIN

**Not too fast.**

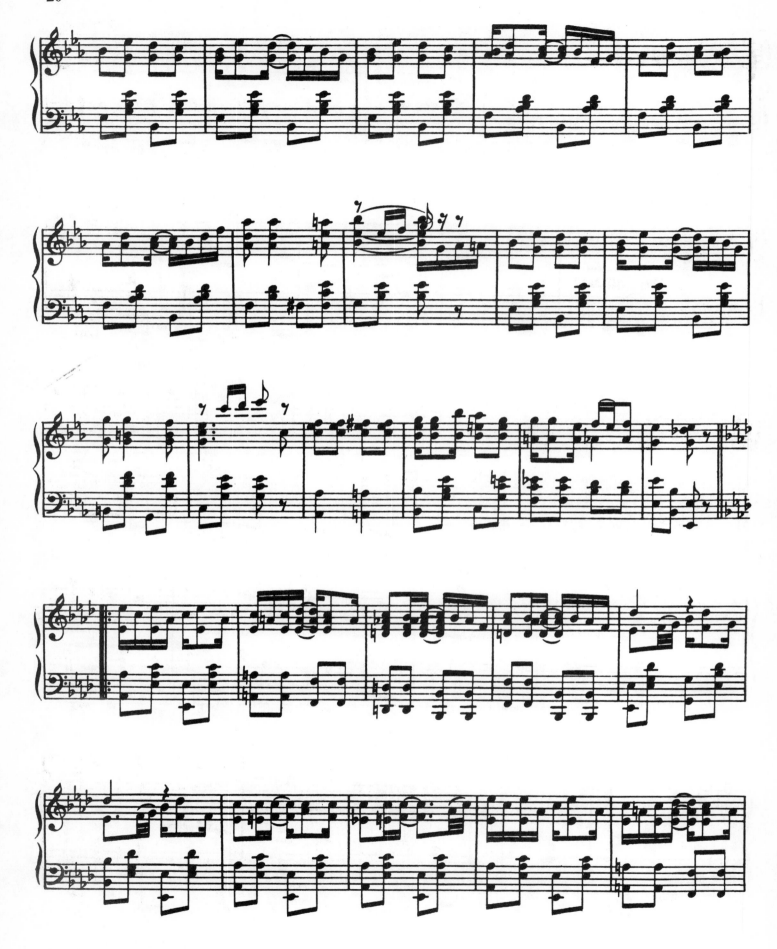

# Weeping Willow

## A Ragtime Two-Step

SCOTT JOPLIN

**Not fast.**

# The Sycamore
## A Concert Rag

SCOTT JOPLIN

*Respectfully dedicated to my friend Tom Turpin*

# The Rose-bud March

SCOTT JOPLIN

**Tempo di Marcia.**

# The Favorite

## A Ragtime Two-Step

SCOTT JOPLIN

# Sun Flower Slow Drag
## A Ragtime Two-Step

SCOTT JOPLIN
and
SCOTT HAYDEN

INTRO.
*Not fast.*

# A Breeze from Alabama

## March and Two-Step

SCOTT JOPLIN

# Elite Syncopations

**Not fast.**

SCOTT JOPLIN

repeat 8va

1.

2.

# The Chrysanthemum

## An Afro-American Intermezzo

SCOTT JOPLIN

# Eugenia

SCOTT JOPLIN

**Slow March Tempo** ♩ = 72

Fine.

# Rag-Time Dance

## A Stop-Time Two-Step

SCOTT JOPLIN

NOTICE: To get the desired effect of "Stop Time," the pianist will please <u>Stamp</u> the heel of one foot heavily upon the floor at the word "Stamp." Do not raise the toe from the floor while stamping.

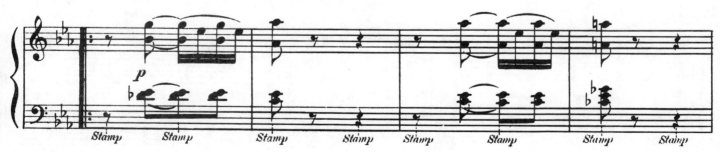

*Stamp*  *Stamp*  *Stamp*  *Stamp*  *Stamp*  *Stamp*  *Stamp*  *Stamp*

58

# Something Doing

### A Ragtime Two-Step

SCOTT JOPLIN
and
SCOTT HAYDEN

**Intro.**
**Not fast.**

Fine.

# Swipesy
**Cakewalk**

SCOTT JOPLIN
and
ARTHUR MARSHALL

*Respectively inscribed to Miss Nellie M. Buttler*

# Sensation
## A Rag

JOSEPH F. LAMB
Arranged by Scott Joplin

# Lily Queen
## A Ragtime Two-Step

SCOTT JOPLIN
and
ARTHUR MARSHALL

# Heliotrope Bouquet

**A Slow Drag Two-Step**

SCOTT JOPLIN
and
LOUIS CHAUVIN

# Combination March

SCOTT JOPLIN

# Bethena
## A Concert Waltz

SCOTT JOPLIN

82

Cantabile.

# The Augustan Club

## Waltzes

SCOTT JOPLIN

INTRODUCTION.

Moderato.

Tempo di Valse.

# Pleasant Moments

**Ragtime Waltz**

SCOTT JOPLIN

# Antoinette
## March and Two-Step

SCOTT JOPLIN

**Tempo di Marcia**

96

TRIO.

# Cleopha

**March and Two-Step**

SCOTT JOPLIN

Ped.　　　　✳　Ped.　　　　✳　Ped.　　　　✳　Ped.　　　　✳　Ped.　　　　✳

# The Crush Collision
## March

SCOTT JOPLIN

106

The noise of the trains while running at the rate of sixty miles per hour,

Whistling for the crossing,

Noise of the trains

Whistle before the collision

The collision

Fine.

# The Strenuous Life

## A Ragtime Two-Step

SCOTT JOPLIN

# Harmony Club
## Waltz

**INTRO.**

SCOTT JOPLIN

**Andante**

# Binks' Waltz

SCOTT JOPLIN

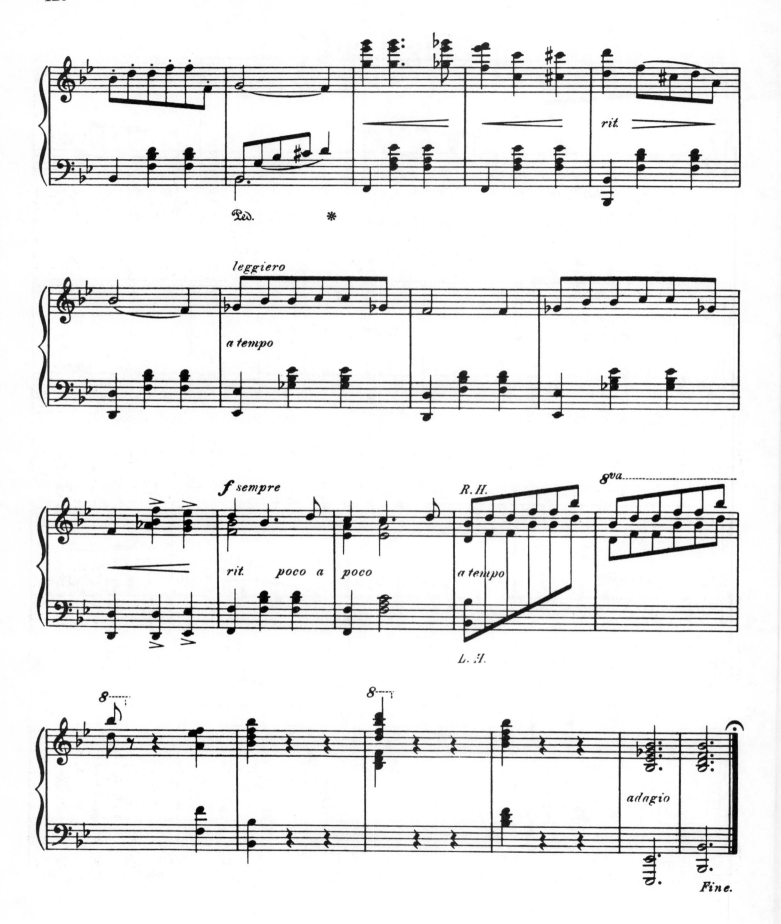

# Fig Leaf

SCOTT JOPLIN

Respectfully dedicated to the Five Musical Spillers.

# Pine Apple Rag

NOTE: Do not play this piece fast.
Composer.

SCOTT JOPLIN

# Solace

## A Mexican Serenade

SCOTT JOPLIN